Grade 1

Scott Foresman
Below-Level Take-Home Readers

ISBN: 0-328-16893-9

Editorial Offices: Glenview, Illinois • Parsippany, New Jersey • New York, New York
Sales Offices: Boston, Massachusetts • Duluth, Georgia • Glenview, Illinois
Coppell, Texas • Sacramento, California • Mesa, Arizona

Contents

How to Use the Take-Home Leveled Readers

1. Tear out the pages for each Take-Home Leveled Reader. Make a copy for each child. Be sure to copy both sides of each page.

2. Fold the pages in half to make a booklet.

3. Staple the pages on the left-hand side.

4. Share the Take-Home Leveled Readers with children. Suggest they read these with family members.

Sam the Duck

by Alan Levine

illustrated by Phyllis Pollema-Cahill

Lexile® and Reading Recovery™ are provided in the Pearson Scott Foresman Leveling Guide.

Genre	Comprehension Skills and Strategy
Realistic fiction	• Character • Draw Conclusions • Monitor and Fix Up

Scott Foresman Reading Street 1.1.1

PEARSON
Scott Foresman

scottforesman.com

ISBN 0-328-13142-3

90000

9 780328 131426

Vocabulary

in

on

way

Word count: 28

Note: The total word count includes words in the running text and headings only. Numerals and words in chapter titles, captions, labels, diagrams, charts, graphs, sidebars, and extra features are not included.

Think and Share

Read Together

1. What does Jack know about Sam? Copy the web on your own paper. Point to the circles as you tell your answers.

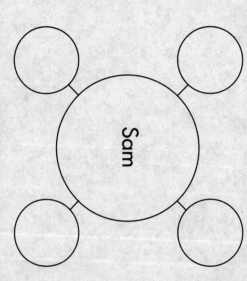

Sam

2. Where does Jack take Sam? Reread the page that tells.

3. Turn to page 4. Find all the short *a* words and say them out loud.

4. Why do you think Jack chose a duck for a pet?

Sam the Duck

by Alan Levine

illustrated by Phyllis Pollema-Cahill

PEARSON

Scott
Foresman

Editorial Offices: Glenview, Illinois • Parsippany, New Jersey • New York, New York
Sales Offices: Needham, Massachusetts • Duluth, Georgia • Glenview, Illinois
Coppell, Texas • Sacramento, California • Mesa, Arizona

All About Ducks

Ducks are living things. They need food and water to live. There are many different kinds of ducks. Ducks live all over the world.

Every effort has been made to secure permission and provide appropriate credit for photographic material. The publisher deeply regrets any omission and pledges to correct errors called to its attention in subsequent editions.

Unless otherwise acknowledged, all photographs are the property of Scott Foresman, a division of Pearson Education.

Photo locators denoted as follows: Top (T), Center (C), Bottom (B), Left (L), Right (R), Background (Bkgd)

Illustrations by Phyllis Pollema-Cahill

Photograph 8 ©Dorling Kindersley

ISBN: 0-328-13142-3

3 4 5 6 7 8 9 10 V010 14 13 12 11 10 09 08 07 06 05

Sam can have a snack.

7

Sam can quack.

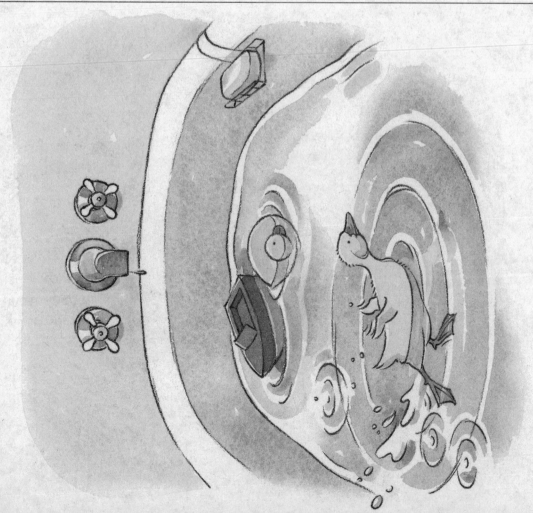

Sam can swim in the tub.

4

Sam can go with Jack.

Sam can see the way
on to the mat.

5

Look at Bix

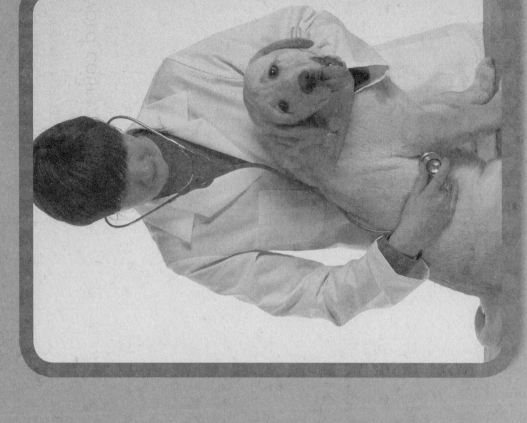

by Shirley Horton

Genre	Comprehension Skills and Strategy
Realistic fiction	• Realism and Fantasy • Sequence • Summarize

Scott Foresman Reading Street 1.1.2

PEARSON
Scott Foresman

scottforesman.com

ISBN 0-328-13145-8

9 780328 131457

90000

Vocabulary

and

take

up

Word count: 25

Think and Share

Read Together

1. Do you think this story could really happen? Why or why not?

2. Tell what happens to Bix from the beginning to the end of the story.

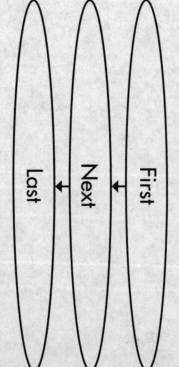

First

Next

Last

3. Find the word in the story that ends in x.

4. If you had a sick pet, like Bix, what would you do?

Look at Bix

by Shirley Horton

Editorial Offices: Glenview, Illinois • Parsippany, New Jersey • New York, New York
Sales Offices: Needham, Massachusetts • Duluth, Georgia • Glenview, Illinois
Coppell, Texas • Sacramento, California • Mesa, Arizona

Medicine for Pets

Some vets make medicine for pets.
Dogs will take medicine that tastes like
cheese. Cats will take medicine that
tastes like fish. Birds will take medicine
that tastes like fruit. What do you think
medicine for rabbits tastes like?

8

Every effort has been made to secure permission and provide appropriate credit for photographic material. The publisher deeply regrets any omission and pledges to correct errors called to its attention in subsequent editions.

Unless otherwise acknowledged, all photographs are the property of Scott Foresman, a division of Pearson Education.

Photo locators denoted as follows: Top (T), Center (C), Bottom (B), Left (L), Right (R), Background (Bkgd)

Opener © Dorling Kindersley; 1 © Dorling Kindersley; 2 © Dorling Kindersley; 3 © Dorling Kindersley; 4 © Dorling Kindersley; 5 © Dorling Kindersley; 6 © Dorling Kindersley; 8 © Dorling Kindersley

ISBN: 0-328-13145-8

© Pearson Education, Inc.

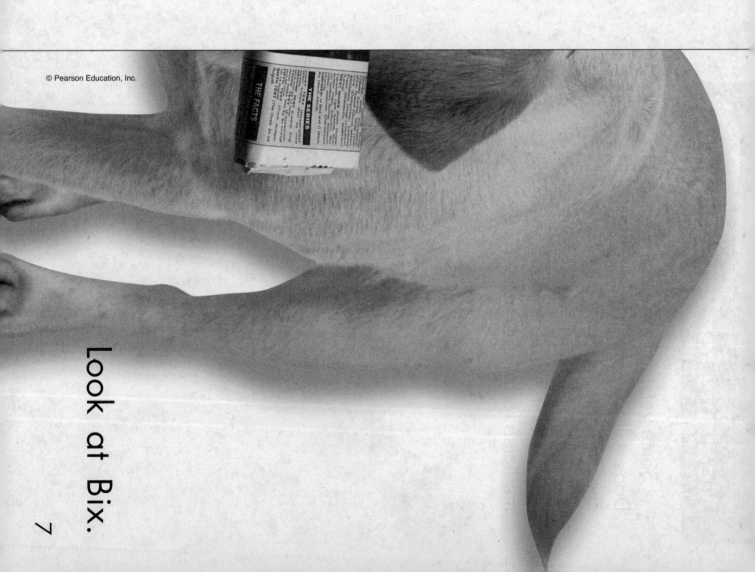

Look at Bix.

7

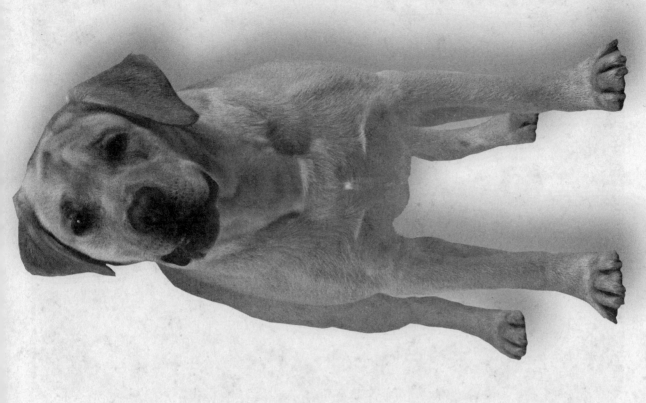

Look at Bix.

Look at Bix take the paper.

Look at Bix up in the van.

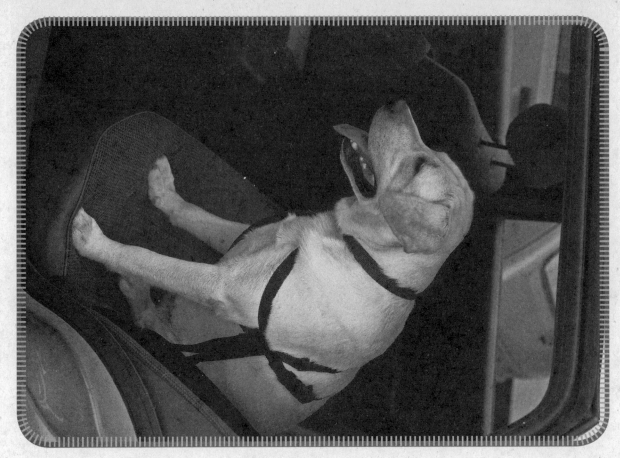

4

Look at Bix and the vet.

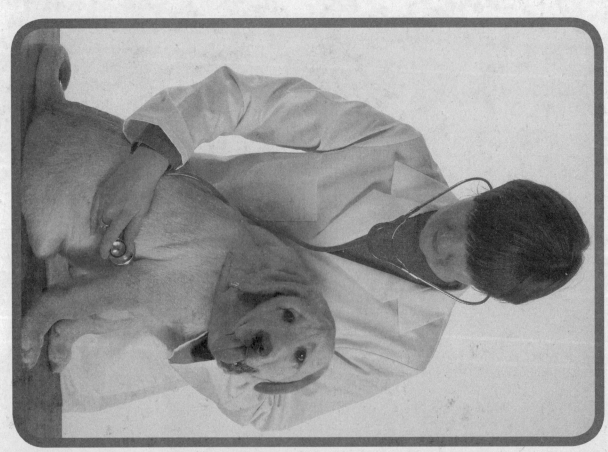

5

Rob, Mom, and Socks

by Kristin Cashore   illustrated by Bob Masheris

Genre	Comprehension Skills and Strategy
Realistic fiction	• Character and Setting • Plot • Visualize

Scott Foresman Reading Street 1.1.3

ISBN 0-328-13148-2

PEARSON
Scott
Foresman

scottforesman.com

Vocabulary

get

help

use

Word count: 44

Note: The total word count includes words in the running text and headings only. Numerals and words in chapter titles, captions, labels, diagrams, charts, graphs, sidebars, and extra features are not included.

Think and Share

Read Together

1. Copy a chart like this one on your own paper. Draw where this story takes place.

Setting

2. What job might Rob, Mom, and Socks use the car for?

3. A plural is a word for more than one thing. Plural words end in s. What plural words can you find in this story?

4. What other kinds of jobs do you think Rob and Socks do on the farm?

Rob, Mom, and Socks

by Kristin Cashore
illustrated by Bob Masheris

PEARSON

Scott
Foresman

Editorial Offices: Glenview, Illinois • Parsippany, New Jersey • New York, New York
Sales Offices: Needham, Massachusetts • Duluth, Georgia • Glenview, Illinois
Coppell, Texas • Sacramento, California • Mesa, Arizona

Farm Dogs

Farm dogs do not have much time to play in the mud! Farm dogs have many jobs. They help the farmer herd the animals. They keep the animals safe from wolves and foxes. They stop animals from eating the crops. Farm dogs are hard workers!

Illustrations by Robert Masheris

Photograph 8 Digital Vision

ISBN: 0-328-13148-2

3 4 5 6 7 8 9 10 V010 14 13 12 11 10 09 08 07 06 05

Rob, Mom, and Socks use the car for a job.

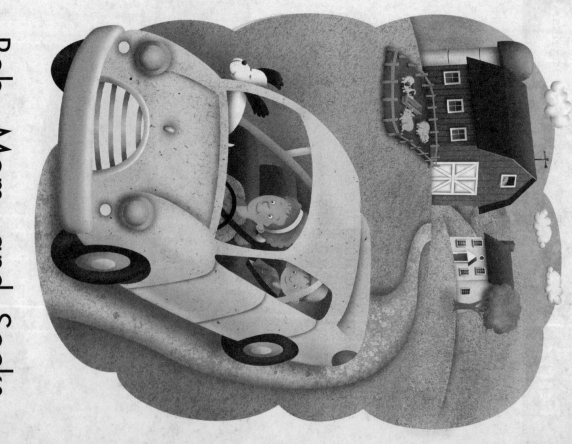

7

Rob and Mom
use rags for a job.

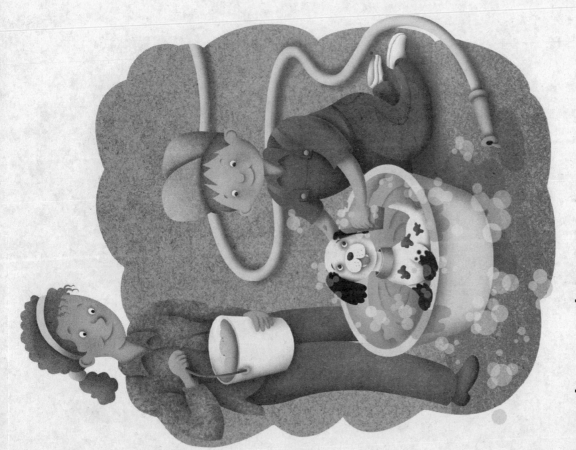

Rob and Mom use soap
to help get Socks clean.

Rob and Mom
use pails for a job.

Rob and Socks
use rocks for a job.

Genre	Comprehension Skills and Strategy	
Realistic fiction	• Realism and Fantasy • Compare and Contrast • Story Structure	

Scott Foresman Reading Street 1.1.5

PEARSON

Scott Foresman

scottforesman.com

ISBN 0-328-13155-5

9 780328 131556

90000

What Animals Do You See?

by Linda B. Ross

illustrated by Phyllis Polema Cahill

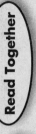

Think and Share (Read Together)

1. Could the kinds of animals in the book really live in the woods?

2. Copy the story chart on your own paper. Tell the characters, setting, and plot of *What Animals Do You See?*

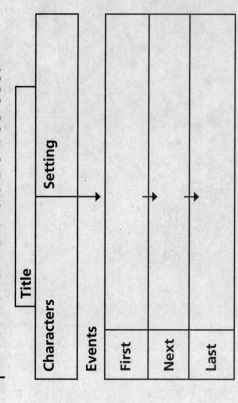

Title	
Characters	Setting

Events	
First	
Next	
Last	

3. Point to the letters in the name *Fran*. Which letter is a vowel and which letters are consonants?

4. What other animals do you think Fran and her family could see on another walk?

Vocabulary

saw

small

tree

your

Word count: 100

Note: The total word count includes words in the running text and headings only. Numerals and words in chapter titles, captions, labels, diagrams, charts, graphs, sidebars, and extra features are not included.

Birds in Nests

Birds live in many different places. No matter where they live, most birds build nests. The mother bird lays her eggs in the nest. She sits on the eggs until they hatch. Then there are baby birds! Soon the baby birds grow up. When they grow up, they will leave the nest.

8

What Animals Do You See?

by Linda B. Ross
illustrated by Phyllis Polema Cahill

Editorial Offices: Glenview, Illinois • Parsippany, New Jersey • New York, New York
Sales Offices: Needham, Massachusetts • Duluth, Georgia • Glenview, Illinois
Coppell, Texas • Ontario, California • Mesa, Arizona

PEARSON

Scott
Foresman

"We saw animals eat dinner,"
said Fran.

"Do you want your dinner?"
said Dad.

"I do!" said Fran.

7

Every effort has been made to secure permission and provide appropriate credit for photographic material. The publisher deeply regrets any omission and pledges to correct errors called to its attention in subsequent editions.

Unless otherwise acknowledged, all photographs are the property of Scott Foresman, a division of Pearson Education.

Photo locators denoted as follows: Top (T), Center (C), Bottom (B), Left (L), Right (R), Background (Bkgd)

Illustrations by Phyllis Polema Cahill

Photograph 8 (B) ©DK Images

ISBN: 0-328-13155-5

2 3 4 5 6 7 8 9 10 V010 14 13 12 11 10 09 08 07 06 05

"Look in the woods," said Mom.
"What do you see?"
"I can see a deer," said Fran.
"He is eating here."

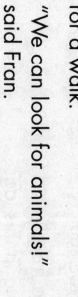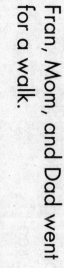

Fran, Mom, and Dad went
for a walk.
"We can look for animals!"
said Fran.

"Look in this log," said Dad.
"What do you see?"

"I can see a frog," said Fran.
"He is eating in this log."

4

"Look in this tree," said Mom.
"What do you see?"

"I can see small birds," said Fran.
"They are eating in the nest!"

5

Time to Eat

by Barbara L. Luciano

illustrated by Ginna Magee

Suggested levels for Guided Reading, DRA,™ Lexile® and Reading Recovery™ are provided in the Pearson Scott Foresman Leveling Guide.

Genre	Comprehension Skills and Strategy
Realistic fiction	• Main Idea • Compare and Contrast • Ask Questions

Scott Foresman Reading Street 1.1.4

PEARSON

Scott Foresman

scottforesman.com

ISBN 0-328-13151-2

90000

9 780328 131518

Vocabulary

eat

her

this

too

Word count: 27

Note: The total word count includes words in the running text and headings only.
Numerals and words in chapter titles, captions, labels, diagrams, charts, graphs,
sidebars, and extra features are not included.

Think and Share

1. What is this story all about?

2. What would you like to ask about the animals on the farm?

3. What endings can you add to the words *eat* and *look*? Copy the chart on your own paper. Write the words with endings in the boxes.

eat	
look	

4. This story takes place at dinnertime. What do you think happens to the animals at other times of the day?

Time to Eat

by Barbara L. Luciano
illustrated by Ginna Magee

PEARSON

Scott
Foresman

Editorial Offices: Glenview, Illinois • Parsippany, New Jersey • New York, New York
Sales Offices: Needham, Massachusetts • Duluth, Georgia • Glenview, Illinois
Coppell, Texas • Sacramento, California • Mesa, Arizona

Read Together

Animals on the Move

All the animals in this book eat. All the animals can move too. Animals have different ways to move. Some animals walk on feet. Some animals use fins to swim. Some animals even hop! What other ways can animals move?

Every effort has been made to secure permission and provide appropriate credit for photographic material. The publisher deeply regrets any omission and pledges to correct errors called to its attention in subsequent editions.

Unless otherwise acknowledged, all photographs are the property of Scott Foresman, a division of Pearson Education.

Photo locators denoted as follows: Top (T), Center (C), Bottom (B), Left (L), Right (R), Background (Bkgd)

Illustrations by Ginna Magee

Photograph 8 Corbis

ISBN: 0-328-13151-2

Copyright © Pearson Education, Inc.

All Rights Reserved. Printed in the United States of America. This publication is protected by Copyright, and permission should be obtained from the publisher prior to any prohibited reproduction, storage in a retrieval system, or transmission in any form by any means, electronic, mechanical, photocopying, recording, or likewise. For information regarding permission(s), write to: Permissions Department, Scott Foresman, 1900 East Lake Avenue, Glenview, Illinois 60025.

3 4 5 6 7 8 9 10 V010 14 13 12 11 10 09 08 07 06 05

Mom and I eat dinner too.

7

The horses eat this dinner.

Mom is looking at her watch.

The chicks eat this dinner.

4

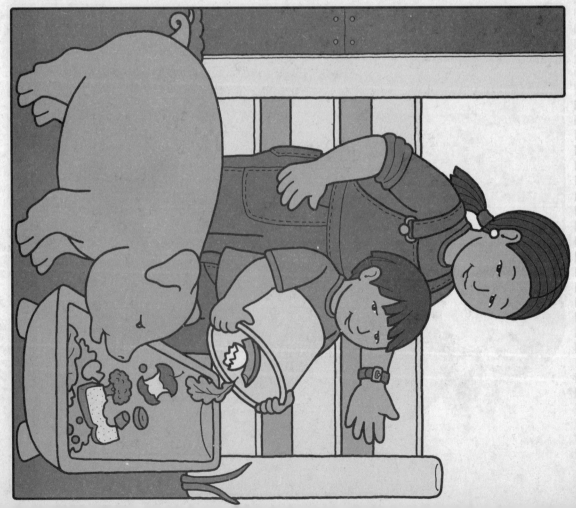

The pig eats this dinner.

5

Life Science

Animals in the Sun

by Donna Foley

Science

Science

Genre	Comprehension Skills and Strategy	
Nonfiction	• Cause and Effect • Author's Purpose • Monitor and Fix Up	

Scott Foresman Reading Street 1.1.6

PEARSON

Scott
Foresman

scottforesman.com

ISBN 0-328-13157-1

90000

9 780328 131570

Vocabulary

home
into
many
them

Word count: 44

Note: The total word count includes words in the running text and headings only. Numerals and words in chapter titles, captions, labels, diagrams, charts, graphs, sidebars, and extra features are not included.

Think and Share   Read Together

1. The animals in the book go into a pond. Why did that happen? Copy the chart onto your own paper and tell the answer.

What happened?
The animals go into a pond.

Why did it happen?

2. Which three animals are named in the book? What do they all do?

3. Find the words in the book with the short *u* sound. Read the words out loud.

4. How many different kinds of animals do you see on page 8?

Animals in the Sun

by Donna Foley

PEARSON
Scott Foresman

Editorial Offices: Glenview, Illinois • Parsippany, New Jersey • New York, New York
Sales Offices: Needham, Massachusetts • Duluth, Georgia • Glenview, Illinois
Coppell, Texas • Sacramento, California • Mesa, Arizona

A pond is the best spot for them.

8

Every effort has been made to secure permission and provide appropriate credit for photographic material. The publisher deeply regrets any omission and pledges to correct errors called to its attention in subsequent editions.

Unless otherwise acknowledged, all photographs are the property of Scott Foresman, a division of Pearson Education.

Photo locators denoted as follows: Top (T), Center (C), Bottom (B), Left (L), Right (R), Background (Bkgd)

Opener Safari/Brand X Pictures; 1 Wild Things/digitalvisiononline.com; 3 Safari/Brand X Pictures; 4 Safari/Brand X Pictures; 5 Safari/Brand X Pictures; 6 Wild Things/digitalvisiononline.com; 7 © Dorling Kindersley; 8 (B) © Dorling Kindersley; 8 (TL) Safari/Brand X Pictures; 8 (CR) Wild Things/digitalvisiononline.com

ISBN: 0-328-13157-1

3 4 5 6 7 8 9 10 V010 14 13 12 11 10 09 08 07 06 05

Many hot zebras go into a pond.

Many hot animals
make their homes here.

Many hot elephants
go into a pond.

Many hot animals
have fun in the sun.

Many hot hippos
go into a pond.

Fun For Families

by Linda B. Ross

Suggested levels for Guided Reading, DRA,™
Lexile,® and Reading Recovery™ are provided
in the Pearson Scott Foresman Leveling Guide.

Social Studies

Social Studies

Genre	Comprehension Skills and Strategy
Nonfiction	• Main Idea • Draw Conclusions • Predict

Scott Foresman Reading Street 1.2.1

PEARSON
Scott
Foresman

scottforesman.com

ISBN 0-328-13160-1

9 780328 131600

90000

Vocabulary

catch

good

no

put

want

Word count: 28

Note: The total word count includes words in the running text and headings only.
Numerals and words in chapter titles, captions, labels, diagrams, charts, graphs,
sidebars, and extra features are not included.

Think and Share Read Together

1. What is *Fun for Families* all about?

2. On page 7, a family is food shopping. What do you think that family will do next? On your own paper, draw a picture of the next thing the family will do. Tell your class about it.

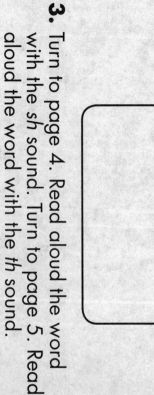

3. Turn to page 4. Read aloud the word with the *sh* sound. Turn to page 5. Read aloud the word with the *th* sound.

4. How many family members can you find in the picture on page 6?

Fun For Families

by Linda B. Ross

PEARSON

Scott Foresman

Editorial Offices: Glenview, Illinois • Parsippany, New Jersey • New York, New York
Sales Offices: Needham, Massachusetts • Duluth, Georgia • Glenview, Illinois
Coppell, Texas • Sacramento, California • Mesa, Arizona

No families skip fun.

8

ISBN: 0-328-13160-1

Copyright © Pearson Education, Inc.

All Rights Reserved. Printed in the United States of America. This publication is protected by Copyright, and permission should be obtained from the publisher prior to any prohibited reproduction, storage in a retrieval system, or transmission in any form by any means, electronic, mechanical, photocopying, recording, or likewise. For information regarding permission(s), write to: Permissions Department, Scott Foresman, 1900 East Lake Avenue, Glenview, Illinois 60025.

3 4 5 6 7 8 9 10 V010 14 13 12 11 10 09 08 07 06 05

Families put food in carts.

7

Families want to have fun.

Families read good books
and talk.

Families catch fish.

4

Families play with a ball.

5

The Play

by Gloria Rose

illustrated by
Luciana Navarro Alves

Suggested levels for Guided Reading, DRA™,
Lexile® and Reading Recovery™ are provided
in the Pearson Scott Foresman Leveling Guide.

Genre	Comprehension Skills and Strategy
Realistic fiction	• Cause and Effect • Main Idea • Monitor and Fix Up

Scott Foresman Reading Street 1.2.2

PEARSON
Scott
Foresman

scottforesman.com

ISBN 0-328-13163-6

9 780328 131631

90000

Vocabulary

be

could

horse

old

paper

Word count: 61

Note: The total word count includes words in the running text and headings only. Numerals and words in chapter titles, captions, labels, diagrams, charts, graphs, sidebars, and extra features are not included.

Think and Share

Read Together

1. Why did the children make costumes and scenery for the stage?

What happened?
The children made costumes and scenery for the stage.

←

Why did it happen?

2. What do Jake and Grace do? Check your answer by looking at the picture on page 5.

3. Make a list of all the characters' names in the story. Which ones have the long *a* sound?

4. Why do the moms and dads on page 7 have happy faces?

The Play
by Gloria Rose

illustrated by
Luciana Navarro Alves

PEARSON
Scott
Foresman

Editorial Offices: Glenview, Illinois • Parsippany, New Jersey • New York, New York
Sales Offices: Needham, Massachusetts • Duluth, Georgia • Glenview, Illinois
Coppell, Texas • Sacramento, California • Mesa, Arizona

Putting on a Play!

Read Together

Many people work together to put on a play. One person is the director. The director tells the actors what to do. Other people make costumes. Others make and paint the scenery. Some helpers turn the stage lights on and off or play music.

Illustrations by Luciana Navarro Alves

ISBN: 0-328-13163-6

Copyright © Pearson Education, Inc.

All Rights Reserved. Printed in the United States of America. This publication is protected by Copyright, and permission should be obtained from the publisher prior to any prohibited reproduction, storage in a retrieval system, or transmission in any form by any means, electronic, mechanical, photocopying, recording, or likewise. For information regarding permission(s), write to: Permissions Department, Scott Foresman, 1900 East Lake Avenue, Glenview, Illinois 60025.

3 4 5 6 7 8 9 10 V010 14 13 12 11 10 09 08 07 06 05

© Pearson Education, Inc.

What could the class do?

The class will put on the play.

7

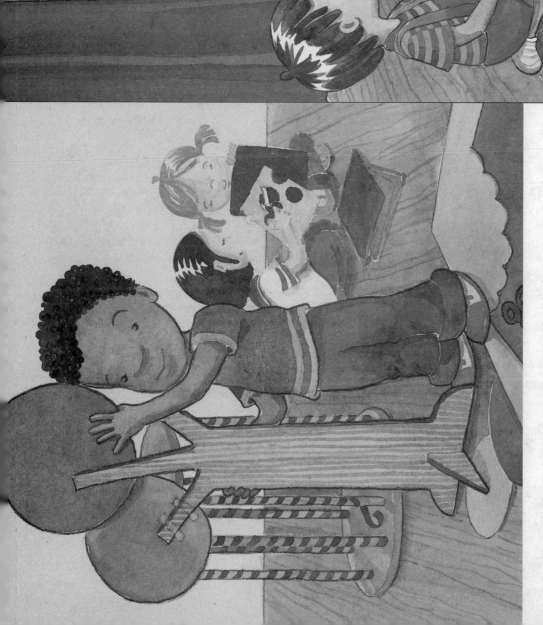

What could Nate do?
Nate will make trees
for the stage.

6

What could the class do?
The class will put on a play.

3

What could Kate do?
Kate will be a yellow bird.

What could Grace and Jake do?
Grace and Jake will make
a horse from old paper.

Social Studies

My
Neighborhood

by Lana Rios

illustrated by Amy Loeffler

Lexile® and Reading Recovery™ are provided in the Pearson Scott Foresman Leveling Guide.

Genre	Comprehension Skills and Strategy	
Nonfiction	• Author's Purpose • Draw Conclusions • Ask Questions	

Scott Foresman Reading Street 1.2.3

PEARSON

Scott
Foresman

scottforesman.com

ISBN 0-328-13166-0

9 780328 131662

90000

Vocabulary

live

out

people

who

work

Word count: 71

Think and Share

1. Why do you think the author wrote this book about her neighborhood?

2. Copy the chart on your paper. Write two questions you have about the book.

My Questions

3. What makes this neighborhood a busy place?

4. What does the picture on page 8 tell about the neighborhood?

My Neighborhood

by Lana Rios

illustrated by Amy Loeffler

PEARSON
Scott Foresman

Editorial Offices: Glenview, Illinois • Parsippany, New Jersey • New York, New York
Sales Offices: Needham, Massachusetts • Duluth, Georgia • Glenview, Illinois
Coppell, Texas • Sacramento, California • Mesa, Arizona

Here is my neighborhood.

It is full of people who

work and play.

8

Illustrations by Amy Loeffler

ISBN: 0-328-13166-0

Copyright © Pearson Education, Inc.

All Rights Reserved. Printed in the United States of America. This publication is protected by Copyright, and permission should be obtained from the publisher prior to any prohibited reproduction, storage in a retrieval system, or transmission in any form by any means, electronic, mechanical, photocopying, recording, or likewise. For information regarding permission(s), write to: Permissions Department, Scott Foresman, 1900 East Lake Avenue, Glenview, Illinois 60025.

3 4 5 6 7 8 9 10 V010 14 13 12 11 10 09 08 07 06 05

Who works in my neighborhood?

Ms. Whit works here and looks out for us.

7

Here is my neighborhood.

People live and work here.

Who works in my neighborhood?

Chuck works here and

drives the bus.

Who lives in my neighborhood?
My pals live here and play ball.

4

Who works in my neighborhood?
Mitch works here and
bakes bread.

5

Life Science

Science

Science

Suggested levels for Guided Reading, DRA,™
Lexile,® and Reading Recovery™ are provided
in the Pearson Scott Foresman Leveling Guide.

We Look at Dinosaurs

by Rhea Alexander
illustrated by Kristen Guerin

Genre	Comprehension Skills and Strategy	
Nonfiction	• Sequence • Cause and Effect • Monitor and Fix Up	

Scott Foresman Reading Street 1.2.4

PEARSON

Scott
Foresman

scottforesman.com

ISBN 0-328-13169-5

9 780328 131693

90000

Think and Share

1. Which kind of dinosaur food does the book talk about first? Which comes next?

First

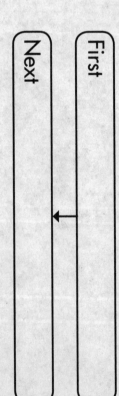

Next

2. Look at the picture on page 3. How do we know that dinosaurs made a home here?

3. Find the contraction that uses the word We as the base.

4. Look at the picture on pages 6 and 7. Point to the dinosaur that ate plants, and then point to the dinosaur that ate meat.

Vocabulary

down
inside
now
there
together

Word count: 62

Note: The total word count includes words in the running text and headings only. Numerals and words in chapter titles, captions, labels, diagrams, charts, graphs, sidebars, and extra features are not included.

We Look at Dinosaurs

by Rhea Alexander

illustrated by Kristen Guerin

Editorial Offices: Glenview, Illinois • Parsippany, New Jersey • New York, New York
Sales Offices: Needham, Massachusetts • Duluth, Georgia • Glenview, Illinois
Coppell, Texas • Sacramento, California • Mesa, Arizona

Dinosaurs don't live now.

But we can still

look at them together.

8

Illustrations by Kristen Guerin.

ISBN: 0-328-13169-5

Copyright © Pearson Education, Inc.

3 4 5 6 7 8 9 10 V010 14 13 12 11 10 09 08 07 06 05

Dinosaurs like this ate meat. We'll look at dinosaurs together.

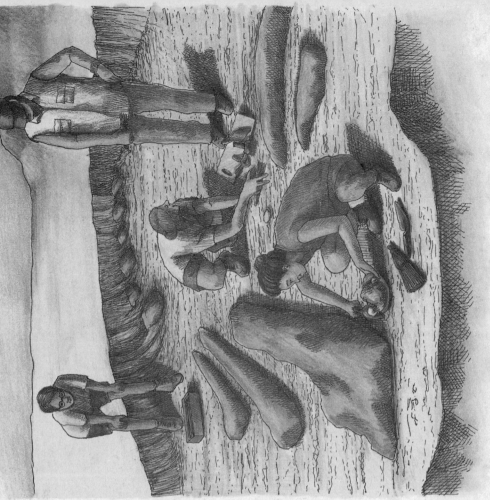

Dinosaurs made a home

down there.

We'll look at dinosaurs together.

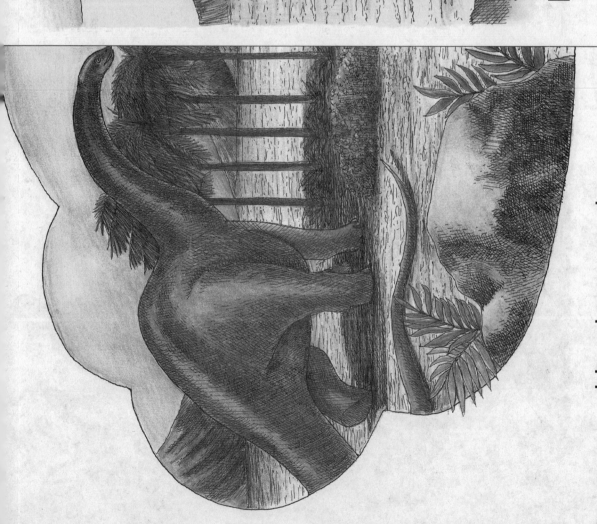

Dinosaurs like this ate plants.

We'll look at dinosaurs together.

Dinosaurs had bones inside.
We'll look at dinosaurs together.

4

Dinosaurs had bones and teeth.
We'll look at dinosaurs together.

5

Earth Science

Science

Science

The Forest

by Rita Crosby

Genre	Comprehension Skills and Strategy
Nonfiction	• Author's Purpose • Cause and Effect • Preview

Scott Foresman Reading Street 1.2.5

PEARSON

Scott
Foresman

scottforesman.com

ISBN 0-328-13172-5

90000

9 780328 131723

Vocabulary

around

find

food

grow

under

water

Word count: 74

Note: The total word count includes words in the running text and headings only. Numerals and words in chapter titles, captions, labels, diagrams, charts, graphs, sidebars, and extra features are not included.

Think and Share

Read Together

1. Why do you think the author wrote about a forest?

2. What did you do to get ready to read this book? How did that help you understand the book better?

3. An -ed ending on an action word means something happened in the past. Which word in the book ends in -ed?

-ed word

4. What did you learn about a forest by looking at the pictures in this book?

The Forest
by Rita Crosby

PEARSON
Scott Foresman

Editorial Offices: Glenview, Illinois • Parsippany, New Jersey • New York, New York
Sales Offices: Needham, Massachusetts • Duluth, Georgia • Glenview, Illinois
Coppell, Texas • Sacramento, California • Mesa, Arizona

We looked around the forest.

We saw a bird in a tree.

8

Every effort has been made to secure permission and provide appropriate credit for photographic material. The publisher deeply regrets any omission and pledges to correct errors called to its attention in subsequent editions.

Unless otherwise acknowledged, all photographs are the property of Scott Foresman, a division of Pearson Education.

Photo locators denoted as follows: Top (T), Center (C), Bottom (B), Left (L), Right (R), Background (Bkgd)

Opener (Bkgd) Digital Vision, Opener (C) Digital Vision; 1 Digital Vision; 3 (CR) © Royalty-Free/Corbis, 3 (CL) Digital Vision, 3 (TL) Getty Images, 3 (BL) Rubberball Productions, 3 (C) © Comstock Inc, 3 (BR) Rubberball Productions; 4 Digital Vision; 5 Digital Vision; 6 © Royalty-Free/Corbis; 7 Digital Vision; 8 (BR) Rubberball Productions, (C) Getty Images

ISBN: 0-328-13172-5

We looked around the forest.

We saw a huge bear find food

under the water.

7

We looked around the forest.

We saw these trees and animals.

We looked around the forest.

We saw a squirrel eat a nut.

We looked around the forest.
We saw trees that grow
green leaves.

4

We looked around the forest.
We saw trees that grow
yellow leaves.

5

Life Science

Science

Science

Worker Bees

by Kristin Cashore

Suggested levels for Guided Reading, DRA™, Lexile®, and Reading Recovery™ are provided in the Pearson Scott Foresman Leveling Guide.

Genre	Comprehension Skills and Strategy
Expository nonfiction	• Compare and Contrast • Sequence • Preview

Scott Foresman Reading Street 1.2.6

ISBN 0-328-13175-X

9 780328 131754

90000

PEARSON

Scott Foresman

scottforesman.com

Vocabulary

also

family

new

other

some

their

Word count: 65

Note: The total word count includes words in the running text and headings only. Numerals and words in chapter titles, captions, labels, diagrams, charts, graphs, sidebars, and extra features are not included.

Think and Share

Read Together

1. Copy the chart on your paper. Draw your home. Draw a bee's home. How are the homes alike and different?

My Home	A Bee's Home

2. What did you do to get ready to read *Worker Bees*? How did that help you understand it?

3. Which words on page 7 have the long e sound?

4. Look at the pictures on page 4. What do the arrows tell you?

Worker Bees
by Kristin Cashore

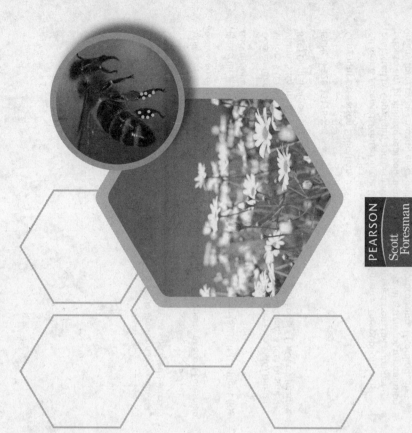

PEARSON
Scott
Foresman

Editorial Offices: Glenview, Illinois • Parsippany, New Jersey • New York, New York
Sales Offices: Needham, Massachusetts • Duluth, Georgia • Glenview, Illinois
Coppell, Texas • Sacramento, California • Mesa, Arizona

Worker bees help their family.
They also help us!

Every effort has been made to secure permission and provide appropriate credit for photographic material. The publisher deeply regrets any omission and pledges to correct errors called to its attention in subsequent editions.

Unless otherwise acknowledged, all photographs are the property of Scott Foresman, a division of Pearson Education.

Photo locators denoted as follows: Top (T), Center (C), Bottom (B), Left (L), Right (R), Background (Bkgd)

Opener (Bkgd) Image Source, Opener (C) John Foxx; 1 (CR) John Foxx, 1 (C) Digital Vision; 3 (C) Digital Vision, 3 (BL) Digital Vision; 4 (T) Digital Vision, 4 (CL) Digital Vision; 5 (C) Image Source; 6 (CR) Digital Vision; 7 (CL) John Foxx, 7 (T) Getty Images; 8 (C) Digital Vision

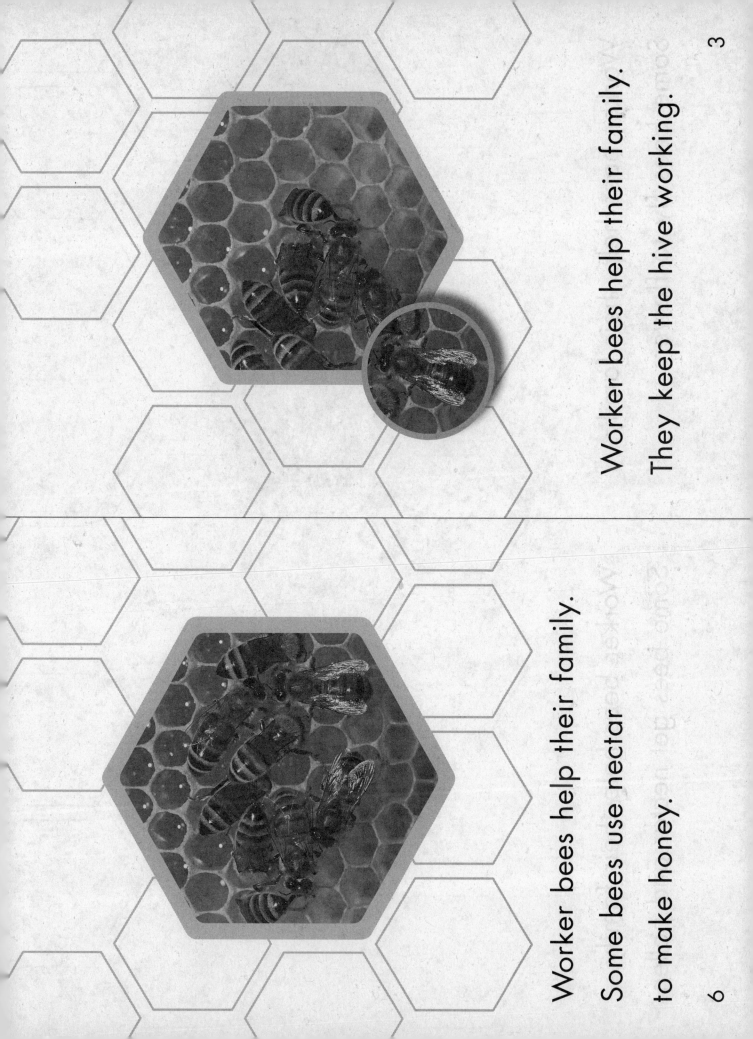

Worker bees help their family.
Worker bees help their family.
They keep the hive working.

3

Worker bees help their family.
Some bees use nectar
to make honey.

6

Worker bees help their family.
Some bees fly to flowers.

4

Worker bees help their family.
Some bees get nectar and pollen.

5

Life Science

Nothing Stays the Same

by Sasha Griffin

illustrated by Ginna Magee

Science

Science

Suggested levels for Guided Reading, DRA,™ Lexile,® and Reading Recovery™ are provided in the Pearson Scott Foresman Leveling Guide.

Genre	Comprehension Skills and Strategy
Nonfiction	• Compare and Contrast • Author's Purpose • Predict

Scott Foresman Reading Street 1.3.1

PEARSON

Scott Foresman

scottforesman.com

Vocabulary

always

become

day

everything

nothing

stays

things

Word count: 86

Note: The total word count includes words in the running text and headings only.
Numerals and words in chapter titles, captions, labels, diagrams, charts, graphs,
sidebars, and extra features are not included.

Think and Share

Read Together

1. How is the boy the same as he was when he was a baby? How is he different? Copy the chart and write your answers.

Same	Different

2. Look at the picture on page 7. What might the boy do next?

3. Find a compound word on page 8. Write the two words that make up a compound word.

4. Look at the pictures in this book. What does the boy look at to find out what he was like as a baby?

Nothing Stays the Same

by Sasha Griffin

illustrated by Ginna Magee

Editorial Offices: Glenview, Illinois • Parsippany, New Jersey • New York, New York
Sales Offices: Needham, Massachusetts • Duluth, Georgia • Glenview, Illinois
Coppell, Texas • Sacramento, California • Mesa, Arizona

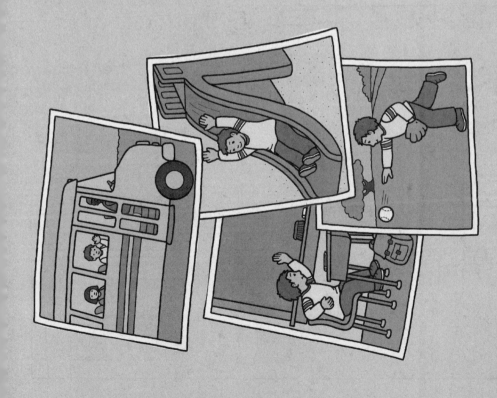

When I was a baby,

I couldn't do everything.

Nothing is the same now that

I have become six.

8

ISBN: 0-328-13178-4

Copyright © Pearson Education, Inc.

All Rights Reserved. Printed in the United States of America. This publication is protected by Copyright, and permission should be obtained from the publisher prior to any prohibited reproduction, storage in a retrieval system, or transmission in any form by any means, electronic, mechanical, photocopying, recording, or likewise. For information regarding permission(s), write to: Permissions Department, Scott Foresman, 1900 East Lake Avenue, Glenview, Illinois 60025.

3 4 5 6 7 8 9 10   V010   14 13 12 11 10 09 08 07 06 05

When I was a baby,
I always slept in the day.
Nothing stays the same.

7

When I was a baby,

I was so small.

Nothing stays the same.

When I was a baby,

I couldn't feed myself.

Nothing stays the same.

When I was a baby,
I couldn't stand.
Nothing stays the same.

When I was a baby,
I would cry for things.
Nothing stays the same.

4

4   5

Can Hank Sing?

by Dale Cooper

illustrated by CD Hullinger

Suggested levels for Guided Reading, DRA™, Lexile® and Reading Recovery™ are provided in the Pearson Scott Foresman Leveling Guide.

Genre	Comprehension Skills and Strategy
Animal fantasy	• Plot
	• Realism and Fantasy
	• Summarize

Scott Foresman Reading Street 1.3.2

PEARSON

Scott Foresman

scottforesman.com

ISBN 0-328-13181-4

90000

9 780328 131815

Vocabulary

any

enough

ever

every

own

sure

were

Word count: 83

Note: The total word count includes words in the running text and headings only. Numerals and words in chapter titles, captions, labels, diagrams, charts, graphs, sidebars, and extra features are not included.

Think and Share (Read Together)

1. What happened at the beginning, at the middle, and at the end of the story?

Beginning
Middle
End

2. Suppose someone had not read this story. Tell the main things that happen.

3. What compound word do you see many times in this book? What two words make the compound word?

4. Hank found that even though his voice was different, he liked it anyway. What is something that is different about you? Do you feel like Hank does?

Can Hank Sing?

by Dale Cooper
illustrated by CD Hullinger

PEARSON
Scott Foresman

Editorial Offices: Glenview, Illinois • Parsippany, New Jersey • New York, New York
Sales Offices: Needham, Massachusetts • Duluth, Georgia • Glenview, Illinois
Coppell, Texas • Sacramento, California • Mesa, Arizona

Your Voice

Read Together

Hank didn't have a voice just like any
other bluebird. Think about your voice.
A person's voice changes over time.
Once you sounded like a baby. Now
you sound like a child. And someday
you will sound like an adult. Think of
how many different ways you will sound
in your life!

8

Every effort has been made to secure permission and provide appropriate credit for photographic material. The publisher deeply regrets any omission and pledges to correct errors called to its attention in subsequent editions.

Unless otherwise acknowledged, all photographs are the property of Scott Foresman, a division of Pearson Education.

Photo locators denoted as follows: Top (T), Center (C), Bottom (B), Left (L), Right (R), Background (Bkgd)

Illustrations by CD Hullinger

Photograph 8 ©DK Images

ISBN: 0-328-13181-4

"Can a bluebird sing like a rooster?" said Hank.

"As long as you sing your own song!" said Jan.

7

"You sing every song so well!"
said Hank.

"Any bluebird can sing," said Jan.

"Are you sure it is a bluebird
song?" said Hank.

"Well, is it your own song?"
said Jan.

"Maybe you were not singing
enough," said Jan.
"But I sing more than ever!"
said Hank.

4

"My song is so little,"
said Hank.
"I think it is a good song,"
said Jan.

5

A Big Move

by Elise Walters

illustrated by Bill Peterson

Suggested levels for Guided Reading, DRA,™ Lexile,® and Reading Recovery™ are provided in the Pearson Scott Foresman Leveling Guide.

Genre	Comprehension Skills and Strategy
Realistic fiction	• Theme • Cause and Effect • Monitor and Fix Up

Scott Foresman Reading Street 1.3.3

PEARSON

Scott Foresman

scottforesman.com

Vocabulary

away

car

friends

house

our

school

very

Word count: 65

Think and Share

1. What is the big idea of this story?

2. What does the family do to get ready for their move?

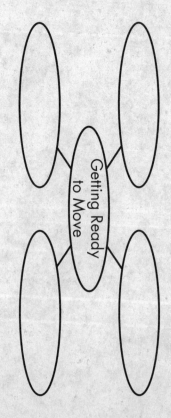

Getting Ready to Move

3. What words from this story end in —es?

4. How would you feel if your family were going to move far away from where you live now?

A Big Move

by Elise Walters

illustrated by Bill Peterson

Editorial Offices: Glenview, Illinois • Parsippany, New Jersey • New York, New York
Sales Offices: Needham, Massachusetts • Duluth, Georgia • Glenview, Illinois
Coppell, Texas • Sacramento, California • Mesa, Arizona

Coming to America

Read Together

People often move from one place to another place. Sometimes these places are close together. But many times people move far away to a whole new country. Millions of people come to the United States from other countries. Many of them arrive first in New York City. When they get there, they are greeted by a famous symbol of freedom, the Statue of Liberty.

Every effort has been made to secure permission and provide appropriate credit for photographic material. The publisher deeply regrets any omission and pledges to correct errors called to its attention in subsequent editions.

Unless otherwise acknowledged, all photographs are the property of Scott Foresman, a division of Pearson Education.

Photo locators denoted as follows: Top (T), Center (C), Bottom (B), Left (L), Right (R), Background (Bkgd)

Illustrations by Bill Peterson

Photograph: 8 Getty Images

ISBN: 0-328-13184-9

Copyright © Pearson Education, Inc.

3 4 5 6 7 8 9 10 V010 14 13 12 11 10 09 08 07 06 05

Mom watches from the car.

Mom and I will miss our friends.

7

Mom saw a very big house
by a school.
Mom and I said it's fine for us.

Mom got a new job.
Mom and I had to move away.

Mom got boxes at a store.
Mom and I packed our things.

4

Mom got some ads.
Mom and I looked for
a new house.

5

The Garden

by Sara Kwan

Illustrated by Amy Loeffler

Genre	Comprehension Skills and Strategy
Realistic fiction	• Plot • Character and Theme • Visualize

Scott Foresman Reading Street 1.3.4

PEARSON

Scott Foresman

scottforesman.com

ISBN 0-328-13187-3

90000

9 780328 131877

Vocabulary

afraid

again

few

how

read

soon

Word count: 107

Note: The total word count includes words in the running text and headings only.
Numerals and words in chapter titles, captions, labels, diagrams, charts, graphs,
sidebars, and extra features are not included.

Think and Share

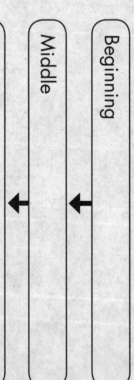

Read Together

1. What happened in the beginning of the story? What happened in the middle? What happened at the end?

Beginning

Middle

End

2. Make a picture in your mind of what the garden looked like in the beginning. How did the garden change?

3. Find the word on page 6 that ends with –ing. Write it on your own paper and circle the base word.

4. How do you think the children felt at the end of the story?

The Garden

by Sara Kwan

Illustrated by Amy Loeffler

PEARSON
Scott
Foresman

Editorial Offices: Glenview, Illinois • Parsippany, New Jersey • New York, New York
Sales Offices: Needham, Massachusetts • Duluth, Georgia • Glenview, Illinois
Coppell, Texas • Sacramento, California • Mesa, Arizona

Growing and Changing

Like other living things, green plants grow and change. Many plants begin as a seed. Seeds need water, the right kind of soil, and the right temperature to grow. If seeds get what they need, roots will grow down to hold the plant in place. The roots get water and food from the soil. A stem grows up toward the sun. Soon leaves will grow from the stem. They will use light from the sun to make food for the plant.

Every effort has been made to secure permission and provide appropriate credit for photographic material. The publisher deeply regrets any omission and pledges to correct errors called to its attention in subsequent editions.

Unless otherwise acknowledged, all photographs are the property of Scott Foresman, a division of Pearson Education.

Photo locators denoted as follows: Top (T), Center (C), Bottom (B), Left (L), Right (R), Background (Bkgd)

Illustrations by Amy Loeffler

Photograph 8 ©DK Images

ISBN: 0-328-13187-3

Copyright © Pearson Education, Inc.

All Rights Reserved. Printed in the United States of America. This publication is protected by Copyright, and permission should be obtained from the publisher prior to any prohibited reproduction, storage in a retrieval system, or transmission in any form by any means, electronic, mechanical, photocopying, recording, or likewise. For information regarding permission(s), write to: Permissions Department, Scott Foresman, 1900 East Lake Avenue, Glenview, Illinois 60025.

3 4 5 6 7 8 9 10 V010 14 13 12 11 10 09 08 07 06 05

A few weeks passed.
"Let's pick our vegetables," said Barb.
The class said it was a good plan.
It was a very good plan.

"I'm afraid our lesson has ended," said Mr. Murk.
"But we will start something new again. How can we find out about plants?"

"Let's start digging and plant the seeds," said Kirk.
The class said it was a good plan. Soon they got started.

"We can read and plant a garden," said Barb.
The class said it was a good plan.
Soon they got started.

4

"Let's draw our garden," said Carl.
The class said it was a good plan.
Soon they got started.

5

Science

Science

Animals Grow and Change

by Bonita Ferraro

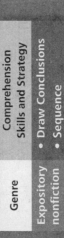

Lexile® and Reading Recovery™ are provided in the Pearson Scott Foresman Leveling Guide.

Genre	Comprehension Skills and Strategy
Expository nonfiction	• Draw Conclusions • Sequence • Text Structure

Scott Foresman Reading Street 1.3.5

ISBN 0-328-13190-3

9 780328 131907

90000

PEARSON

Scott
Foresman

scottforesman.com

Think and Share

1. This book shows that all animals, such as birds, gerbils, tadpoles, and caterpillars, grow and change. What do you think will happen to a baby rabbit as time passes?

2. Copy the chart on your own paper. Draw pictures in the boxes to show how a caterpillar changes as it grows. Reread page 8 to check the order.

First	Next	Last
caterpillar	pupa	butterfly

3. Find the contraction on page 5. On your paper, write the two words that make up the contraction.

4. Turn to page 7. What do the pictures show about what happens to a tadpole?

Vocabulary

done
know
push
visit
wait

Word count: 122

Note: The total word count includes words in the running text and headings only. Numerals and words in chapter titles, captions, labels, diagrams, charts, graphs, sidebars, and extra features are not included.

Animals Grow and Change

by Bonita Ferraro

PEARSON
Scott
Foresman

Editorial Offices: Glenview, Illinois • Parsippany, New Jersey • New York, New York
Sales Offices: Needham, Massachusetts • Duluth, Georgia • Glenview, Illinois
Coppell, Texas • Sacramento, California • Mesa, Arizona

Look at the caterpillar.
Wait for time to pass.
It is a pupa in a chrysalis.
Then it turns into a butterfly.

Every effort has been made to secure permission and provide appropriate credit for photographic material. The publisher deeply regrets any omission and pledges to correct errors called to its attention in subsequent editions.

Unless otherwise acknowledged, all photographs are the property of Scott Foresman, a division of Pearson Education.

Photo locators denoted as follows: Top (T), Center (C), Bottom (B), Left (L), Right (R), Background (BKgd)

Opener (CL) Creatas, Opener (BC) Creatas; 1 (BC) Creatas, 1 (TL) Creatas; 3 (TL) Getty Images, 3 (BL) Getty Images, 3 (TR) Getty Images, 3 (BR) Getty Images; 4 (T) Peter Chadwick/DK Images, 4 (TL) Patti Murray/Animals Animals/Earth Scenes, 4 (BR) EA & RW Schreiber/Animals/Earth Scenes; 5 (T) Getty Images, 5 (C) Getty Images; 6 (T) Jerome Wexler/Visuals Unlimited, 6 (C) Getty Images; 7 (T) Frank Greenaway/DK Images; 8 (TR) Creatas, 8 (TL) Creatas, 8 (CL) Creatas, 8 (BR) Creatas

ISBN: 0-328-13190-3

© Pearson Education, Inc.

Look at the baby tadpole.
At first, it looks like a fish.
Wait for time to pass.
The tadpole will turn into a frog.

7

Do you know that animals grow
and change?
A kitten and a puppy do.
Let's visit some other animals.

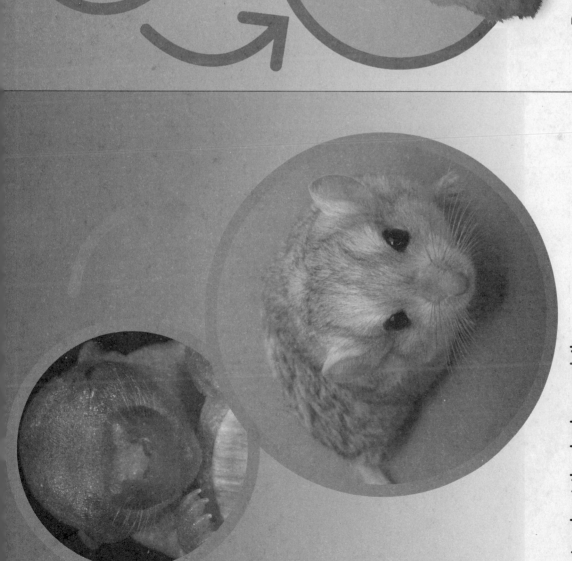

Look at the baby gerbil.
It is not done growing.
Wait for time to pass.
The gerbil will get big and grow fur.

Look at the baby bird.
Baby birds crawl out of eggs.
Wait for time to pass.

4

The birds will grow and change.
They've got feathers now.
The birds will push off and fly away.

5

Earth Science

Seasons Change

by Beth Wells

Science

Science

Genre	Comprehension Skills and Strategy	
Nonfiction	• Sequence • Draw Conclusions • Prior Knowledge	

Scott Foresman Reading Street 1.3.6

PEARSON
Scott
Foresman

scottforesman.com

ISBN 0-328-13193-8

90000

9 780328 131938

Vocabulary

before
does
good-bye
oh
right
won't

Word count: 80

Think and Share

Read Together

1. What season comes after fall?

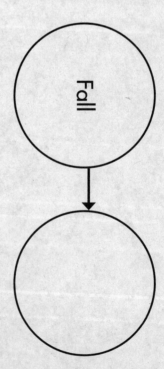

Fall

2. Think about spring where you live. What did you know about spring before you read this book?

3. Find the word in this book that has a hyphen. Write the word on your paper. How many times did you find the word in this book?

4. How do you think the sky looks on a day like the picture on page 8?

Seasons Change
by Beth Wells

PEARSON
Scott
Foresman

Editorial Offices: Glenview, Illinois • Parsippany, New Jersey • New York, New York
Sales Offices: Needham, Massachusetts • Duluth, Georgia • Glenview, Illinois
Coppell, Texas • Sacramento, California • Mesa, Arizona

How does it feel outside today?
The weather could be just right!
But it won't stay the same.
Seasons change!

Every effort has been made to secure permission and provide appropriate credit for photographic material. The publisher deeply regrets any omission and pledges to correct errors called to its attention in subsequent editions.

Unless otherwise acknowledged, all photographs are the property of Scott Foresman, a division of Pearson Education.

Photo locators denoted as follows: Top (T), Center (C), Bottom (B), Left (L), Right (R), Background (Bkgd)

Opener (CL) Digital Vision, Opener (BL) Brand X Pictures, Opener (BR) Brand X Pictures, Opener (CR) © Image Source/Superstock; 1 Image Ideas; 3 (TL) Digital Vision, 3 (BL) Brand X Pictures, 3 (BR) Brand X Pictures, 3 (TR) © Image Source/Superstock; 4 (C) Digital Vision, 4 (TL) Brand X Pictures, 4 (BL) Corel; 5 (C) © Image Source/Superstock, 5 (TR) Brand X Pictures, 5 (BR) © Frank Siteman/Index Stock Images; 6 (C) Brand X Pictures, 6 (TR) Brand X Pictures, 6 (CR) © Royalty-Free/Corbis, 6 (BR) Peter Pearson/ Getty Images; 7 (C) Brand X Pictures, 7 (T) Getty Images, 7 (BL) Corel; 8 Image Ideas

ISBN: 0-328-13193-8

3 4 5 6 7 8 9 10 V010 14 13 12 11 10 09 08 07 06 05

Good-bye, fall!
Winter is here.
It's the coldest time of all.

Weather helps us learn about
the seasons.
Does it always feel the same outside?
Oh no, not when the seasons
change.

Good-bye, summer!
Fall is here.
It's cooler now.

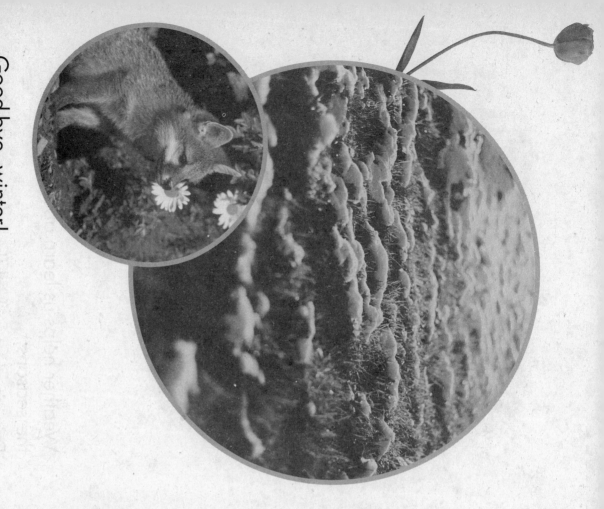

Good-bye, winter!
Spring is here.
It's warmer than before.

4

Good-bye, spring!
Summer is here.
It's the hottest time of all.

4

5

A Party for Pedro

by Maria Santos

illustrated by Mike Dammer

Genre	Comprehension Skills and Strategy
Realistic fiction	• Draw Conclusions • Author's Purpose • Monitor and Fix Up

Scott Foresman Reading Street 1.4.1

PEARSON
Scott
Foresman

scottforesman.com

ISBN 0-328-13196-2

90000

9 780328 131969

Vocabulary

about

enjoy

gives

surprise

surprised

worry

would

Word count: 87

Note: The total word count includes words in the running text and headings only. Numerals and words in chapter titles, captions, labels, diagrams, charts, graphs, sidebars, and extra features are not included.

Think and Share

Read Together

1. Do you think Pedro had fun at his party? How does the story let you know how he feels?

2. As you read the part of the book about the piñata, did you know what it was? If not, what did you do to figure out what it was?

3. Make a chart like the one below. Look back in the story and find words that have the long a sound spelled ay or ai and words that show possession. Write the words in the right place on the chart.

ay	ai	's

4. Look back at page 5. What kinds of treats might be in Pedro's piñata?

A Party for Pedro

by Maria Santos

illustrated by Mike Dammer

PEARSON

Scott Foresman

Editorial Offices: Glenview, Illinois • Parsippany, New Jersey • New York, New York
Sales Offices: Needham, Massachusetts • Duluth, Georgia • Glenview, Illinois
Coppell, Texas • Ontario, California • Mesa, Arizona

Piñatas from Mexico

Piñatas can come in many shapes, sizes, and colors. They are filled with candy and other treats. Piñatas have been around in Mexico for a long time. In the United States, breaking a piñata has become a tradition at many birthday parties.

8

8 ©Jim Gaigmyle/Corbis

ISBN: 0-328-13196-2

2 3 4 5 6 7 8 9 10 V010 14 13 12 11 10 09 08 07 06 05

A band plays, and everyone dances.
"I knew this would be a good day,"
Pedro says. "Thanks, Mom."

Today is Pedro's birthday.
"I can't wait," Pedro says. "Will
everything be OK?"
"Don't worry," says Mom.

It is about time to eat. Grandma's
tacos are the best.

Suddenly everyone yells, "Surprise!" Pedro laughs, and his mom gives him a large box. He is surprised by all the toys inside.

The children play a piñata game. Pedro hits it, and it breaks. Treats rain down for everyone to enjoy.

Reach for Your Dreams

by Winston White

illustrated by Donna Catanese

Genre	Comprehension Skills and Strategy	
Realistic fiction	• Theme • Realism and Fantasy • Graphic Organizer	

Scott Foresman Reading Street 1.4.2

PEARSON

Scott Foresman

scottforesman.com

ISBN 0-328-13199-7

9 780328 131990

90000

Vocabulary

colors
draw
drew
great
over
show
sign

Word count: 115

Note: The total word count includes words in the running text and headings only. Numerals and words in chapter titles, captions, labels, diagrams, charts, graphs, sidebars, and extra features are not included.

Think and Share

Read Together

1. What is the big idea of this story?

2. Make a story map about what happened in this story. Tell what happened at the beginning, the middle, and the end of this story.

Title: Reach for Your Dreams

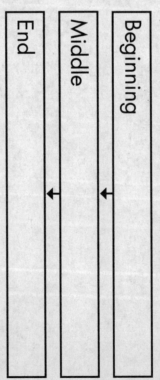

Beginning
Middle
End

3. What vowel sound do you hear in both reach and dream? Find other words in the story that have the same sound.

4. What special talent do you have? Tell about it.

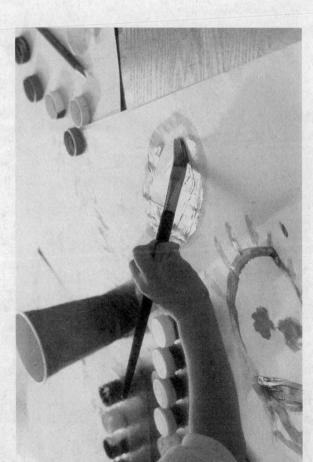

Becoming an Artist

Becoming an artist means following your dreams. Tomie dePaola always wanted to write books. He also wanted to draw the pictures for the books. He wrote a lot and drew a lot when he was in school. Now that he is grown up, Tomie writes and draws children's books. You may have read some of his books. One of his books is called *Strega Nona*. Tomie dePaola followed his dreams.

Reach for Your Dreams

by Winston White

illustrated by Donna Catanese

PEARSON
Scott Foresman

Editorial Offices: Glenview, Illinois • Parsippany, New Jersey • New York, New York
Sales Offices: Needham, Massachusetts • Duluth, Georgia • Glenview, Illinois
Coppell, Texas • Ontario, California • Mesa, Arizona

"Look over here and let's read this sign," said Miss Jean. "How can you reach your dream?"

7

"I am Miss Jean," said the camp counselor. "Welcome to Camp Dream."

"I play sports," said Jess. "I can kick a ball very far. My dream is to be on a great soccer team."

4

Miss Jean and the campers sat by the fire.

"Tell me what you like to do," said Miss Jean.

"I like to cook," said Dean. "I dream of being a great cook one day."

4

5

"I can draw!" Sam cried. "I drew this with a lot of colors. I will be a great artist one day. I will have a show with all my drawings."

Earth Science

Science

Science

Dinosaur Bones Don't Rot

by Dale Cooper
illustrated by Nicole Wong

Genre	Comprehension Skills and Strategy
Expository nonfiction	• Author's Purpose • Cause and Effect • Monitor and Fix-Up

Scott Foresman Reading Street 1.4.3

ISBN 0-328-13202-0

9 780328 132027

90000

PEARSON

Scott
Foresman

scottforesman.com

Vocabulary

found

mouth

once

took

wild

Word count: 147

Note: The total word count includes words in the running text and headings only. Numerals and words in chapter titles, captions, labels, diagrams, charts, graphs, sidebars, and extra features are not included.

Think and Share

Read Together

1. Think about this book. Why do you think the writer wrote this book? What did the writer want you to learn?
2. Scientists learn about dinosaurs from their bones. Read about two kinds of dinosaurs. Write one fact that you learned about each dinosaur. Use the chart below to make your list.

Dinosaur	Fact
1.	
2.	

3. Write all the words in this book that end with *–ed*. Circle each base word.
4. Turn back to page 7. Look at the picture. What is happening in the picture?

Dinosaur Bones Don't Rot

by Dale Cooper • illustrated by Nicole Wong

PEARSON

Scott Foresman

Editorial Offices: Glenview, Illinois • Parsippany, New Jersey • New York, New York
Sales Offices: Needham, Massachusetts • Duluth, Georgia • Glenview, Illinois
Coppell, Texas • Ontario, California • Mesa, Arizona

We have found many dinosaur bones. More are still under the ground. Maybe they are under our roads and houses. Who knows? They could be under your school!

Every effort has been made to secure permission and provide appropriate credit for photographic material. The publisher deeply regrets any omission and pledges to correct errors called to its attention in subsequent editions.

Unless otherwise acknowledged, all photographs are the property of Scott Foresman, a division of Pearson Education.

ISBN: 0-328-13202-0

2 3 4 5 6 7 8 9 10 V010 14 13 12 11 10 09 08 07 06 05

People found the bones and dug them up. They took them to museums. The bones tell us that T-Rex had a strong mouth with sharp teeth.

Many years later, the water dried up.
The land got higher. The bones were
pushed to the top of the land.

Long ago, wild dinosaurs like this
T-Rex walked all over the Earth. How
do we know? We have found many
dinosaur bones.

We have found dinosaur bones where there was once water. When a dinosaur died, water covered it up. Then the body rotted. Only the bones were left.

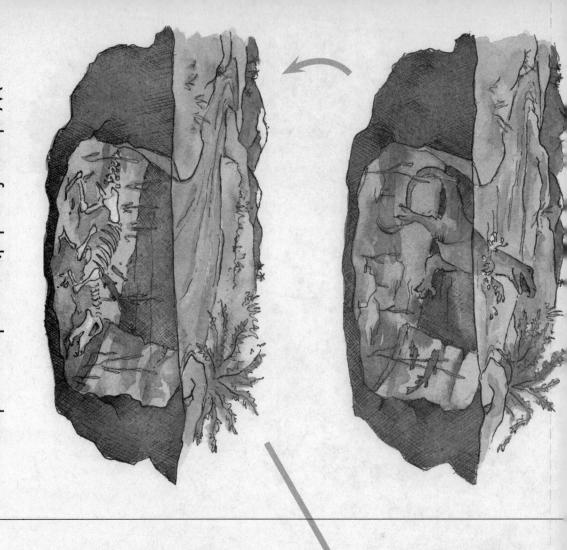

As time went by, sand and mud filled the spaces around the bones. After a long time, the sand and mud became rock.

The Moon Festival

by Gloria Rose

illustrated by Janet Nelson

Genre	Comprehension Skills and Strategy
Realistic fiction	• Realism and Fantasy • Plot • Monitor and Fix-Up

Scott Foresman Reading Street 1.4.4

PEARSON

Scott
Foresman

scottforesman.com

ISBN 0-328-13205-5

9 780328 132058

90000

Vocabulary

above

eight

laugh

moon

touch

Word count: 202

Think and Share

1. Could this story happen in real life? Tell why you think as you do.

2. You read about the Moon Festival. If you did not know what the Moon Festival is, how could you find out more about it?

3. Mai gives a happy laugh after she makes her wish. Show how you laugh when you are happy.

4. Use a diagram like the one below to show how Moon Festival and Thanksgiving are alike and different.

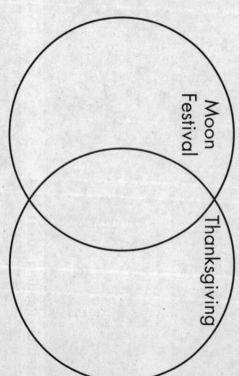

Moon Festival   Thanksgiving

The Moon Festival

by Gloria Rose   illustrated by Janet Nelson

PEARSON

Scott
Foresman

Editorial Offices: Glenview, Illinois • Parsippany, New Jersey • New York, New York
Sales Offices: Needham, Massachusetts • Duluth, Georgia • Glenview, Illinois
Coppell, Texas • Ontario, California • Mesa, Arizona

Read Together

Moon Cakes and the Moon Festival

The Chinese Moon Festival is a little like Thanksgiving. It is celebrated at the end of the harvest season. On this day, Chinese families gather together. They tell the story about a lady who lived in the moon. They give each other small, round moon cakes. Some moon cakes have a yellow egg yolk in the middle. The yolk looks like a bright, full moon!

8

Every effort has been made to secure permission and provide appropriate credit for photographic material. The publisher deeply regrets any omission and pledges to correct errors called to its attention in subsequent editions.

Unless otherwise acknowledged, all photographs are the property of Scott Foresman, a division of Pearson Education.

8 ©Jim Richardson/CORBIS

ISBN: 0-328-13205-5

Mai looked at the moon cakes. She made the same wish she had made all day. Then she gave a happy laugh. She knew her wish would soon come true!

It was the day of the Moon Festival.
Mai's whole family was coming
for dinner.
"Did you get moon cakes?"
Mai asked.

The family ate dinner together.
Grandfather told the story about a lady
who lived in the moon.
"We can each make a wish," he said.

4

"I want moon cakes," cried Mai.
"We have eight moon cakes,"
said Mother. "But it's wrong
to touch them now. We must make
dinner first."

"We'll tie lights above us like more
moons," said Mother. "We will say
thank you for all we have."
"I will say thank you for moon cakes,"
thought Mai.

5

A Good Big Brother

by Libby McCord

illustrated by Doreen Gay Kassel

Genre	Comprehension Skills and Strategy
Realistic fiction	• Character, Setting, Plot • Realism and Fantasy • Story Structure

Scott Foresman Reading Street 1.4.5

PEARSON

Scott Foresman

scottforesman.com

Vocabulary

picture

remember

room

stood

thought

Word count: 216

Think and Share

Read Together

1. Who is Marco? Who are the other characters in this story?

2. How does Marco feel about a baby brother in the beginning of the story? How does he feel at the end?

3. Write a sentence or two using the words room, picture, and remember.

4. If you had a new brother or sister, how would you help?

A Good Big Brother

by Libby McCord

illustrated by Doreen Gay Kassel

Editorial Offices: Glenview, Illinois • Parsippany, New Jersey • New York, New York
Sales Offices: Needham, Massachusetts • Duluth, Georgia • Glenview, Illinois
Coppell, Texas • Ontario, California • Mesa, Arizona

A Care Book

Make a picture album of people you love and care about. It can hold photographs of you and your family. Or, it can be a book of your drawings of people you love. You can call it your Care Book.

Think about the people you love most. Find pictures or make some of yourself doing things you like with your family or friends. Write the names of everybody in your pictures. Make up sentences about what you are doing in the pictures.

Take your Care Book home. Show it to all the people you love.

ISBN: 0-328-13208-X

Copyright © Pearson Education, Inc.

All Rights Reserved. Printed in the United States of America. This publication is protected by Copyright, and permission should be obtained from the publisher prior to any prohibited reproduction, storage in a retrieval system, or transmission in any form by any means, electronic, mechanical, photocopying, recording, or likewise. For information regarding permission(s), write to: Permissions Department, Scott Foresman, 1900 East Lake Avenue, Glenview, Illinois 60025.

2 3 4 5 6 7 8 9 10 V010 14 13 12 11 10 09 08 07 06 05

This is my baby brother. He is cute.
I share my dad's lap with my brother.
I am a good big brother.

7

I am Marco. This is my dad.
See the picture? That is my family.
Soon, we will have a new baby.

This is my bedroom. "Where will
the baby sleep?" I asked.
"In your room with you," said Dad.
"I remember when I stood at the door
to watch you sleep."

This is my mom. She spends lots of time with me.

"Will she still have time with the new baby?" I thought.

"Mom, will you still take me to the park?" I asked.

"I will take you and the baby to the park," Mom said.

Does a Babysitter Know What to Do?

by Rose Valdez

illustrated by Freddie Levin

Suggested levels for Guided Reading, DRA,™
Lexile,® and Reading Recovery™ are provided
in the Pearson Scott Foresman Leveling Guide.

Genre	Comprehension Skills and Strategy
Narrative nonfiction	• Cause and Effect • Main Idea • Preview the Text

Scott Foresman Reading Street 1.4.6

PEARSON
Scott
Foresman

scottforesman.com

ISBN 0-328-13211-X

9 780328 132119

90000

Vocabulary

across

because

dance

only

opened

shoes

told

Word count: 177

Note: The total word count includes words in the running text and headings only. Numerals and words in chapter titles, captions, labels, diagrams, charts, graphs, sidebars, and extra features are not included.

Think and Share

Read Together

1. Why does the boy need a babysitter?

2. Before you read the book, what could you do to tell what it might be about?

3. In this book the boy wants to dance, and the mother opened a store. Show someone what dance means. Did the mother start a new business or go out of business?

4. What did you learn from this book about having a babysitter?

Does a Babysitter Know What to Do?

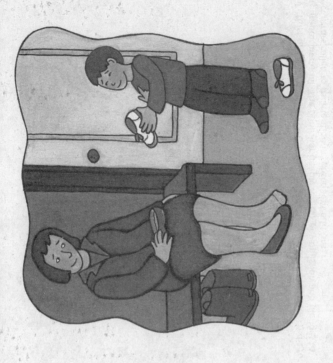

by Rose Valdez   illustrated by Freddie Levin

PEARSON

Scott
Foresman

Editorial Offices: Glenview, Illinois • Parsippany, New Jersey • New York, New York
Sales Offices: Needham, Massachusetts • Duluth, Georgia • Glenview, Illinois
Coppell, Texas • Ontario, California • Mesa, Arizona

We open the door. It is the babysitter!

I think I will like him. He looks like he likes games. And I bet he likes snacks too. I think I will have fun after all!

8

© Pearson Education, Inc.

Hey! I like to play games! I like to eat snacks!

7

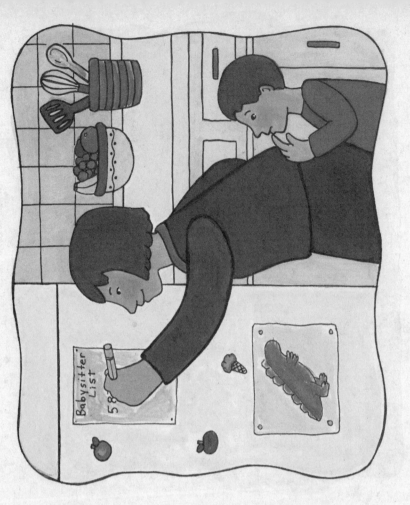

My mom opened her own store. Now she goes to work. A babysitter will stay with me.
My mom says the babysitter is nice. The babysitter lives across the street.

My mom tells me the babysitter will play any game I want to play. She says the babysitter will give me a snack as well.

4

I am not so sure about this.
Does a babysitter know what to do?
Will she let me dance across the room?
What if my tooth falls out? What if I
can't sleep because I am thirsty?

I told my mom that I want to put my
shoes on too. I could go with her.
My mom said that she will be gone
only for a short time. She said the time
will go by quickly.

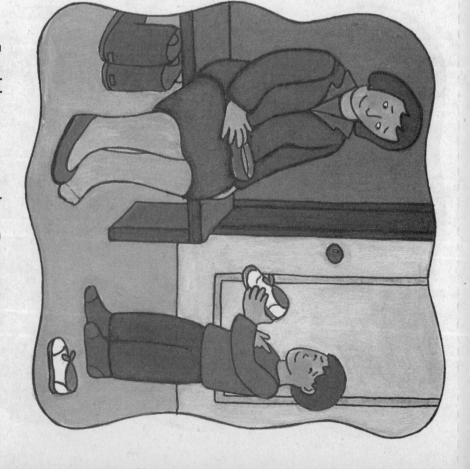

5

What the Dog Saw

by Gregory Grissom
illustrated by Mike Dammer

Suggested levels for Guided Reading, DRA,
Lexile,® and Reading Recovery™ are provided
in the Pearson Scott Foresman Leveling Guide.

Genre	Comprehension Skills and Strategy
Animal fantasy	• Character, Setting, Plot • Realism and Fantasy • Story Structure

Scott Foresman Reading Street 1.5.1

PEARSON

Scott
Foresman

scottforesman.com

Vocabulary

along

behind

eyes

never

pulling

toward

Word count: 131

Note: The total word count includes words in the running text and headings only. Numerals and words in chapter titles, captions, labels, diagrams, charts, graphs, sidebars, and extra features are not included.

Think and Share Read Together

1. Where does this story take place?

2. Think about what happened in this story. Now explain what Brown sees the other animals do. Organize your ideas in a 3-column chart like the one below.

squirrel	ant	bird

3. Which animal *pulled* her food?

4. Why do you think it is easier for Brown to eat than it is for the other animals to eat? Explain your answer.

What the Dog Saw

by Gregory Grissom
illustrated by Mike Dammer

PEARSON
Scott
Foresman

Editorial Offices: Glenview, Illinois • Parsippany, New Jersey • New York, New York
Sales Offices: Needham, Massachusetts • Duluth, Georgia • Glenview, Illinois
Coppell, Texas • Ontario, California • Mesa, Arizona

Plants and Animals Work Together

Plants and animals help each other. Plants and animals keep each other alive! Plants help the animals. Squirrels like to eat nuts and seeds. Ants like to eat fruit and sweet things. Birds like fruit and seeds.

Animals also help the plants. Animals carry seeds around. They drop seeds all over the place. The seeds grow into plants. Animals help make sure that plants grow in lots of places!

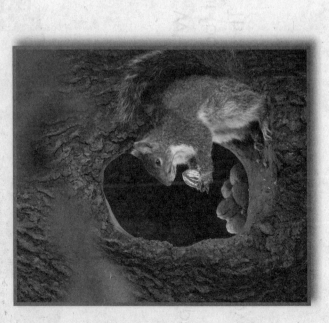

8

Every effort has been made to secure permission and provide appropriate credit for photographic material. The publisher deeply regrets any omission and pledges to correct errors called to its attention in subsequent editions.

Unless otherwise acknowledged, all photographs are the property of Scott Foresman, a division of Pearson Education.

ISBN: 0-328-13214-4

When I am hungry, my owner puts out food! I am a lucky dog! Thanks for visiting. I will eat now.

7

Hi! My name is Brown. Can you guess why that is my name? I live behind the house. All kinds of things go on out here. Watch with me.

Look at that bird.
That bird found an apple. She is flying toward her nest. Look at her eyes! Is the apple too heavy? Wow! She must be hungry.

4

Look at the squirrel!
His arms are full of nuts. I have never
seen so many nuts. What makes his
cheeks so round? Nuts!
Wow! He must be hungry!

© Pearson Education, Inc.

Look at that ant.
What is she pulling along? It is very
big. It is a huge pear!
Wow! She must be hungry!

5

Fly Away

by Ronda Greenberg

illustrated by Chad Thompson

Suggested levels for Guided Reading, DRA,™
Lexile,® and Reading Recovery™ are provided
in the Pearson Scott Foresman Leveling Guide.

Genre	Comprehension Skills and Strategy
Realistic fiction	• Sequence • Cause and Effect • Summarize

Scott Foresman Reading Street 1.5.2

PEARSON

Scott
Foresman

scottforesman.com

ISBN 0-328-13217-9

Vocabulary

door
loved
should
wood

Word count: 195

Note: The total word count includes words in the running text and headings only. Numerals and words in chapter titles, captions, labels, diagrams, charts, graphs, sidebars, and extra features are not included.

Think and Share

Read Together

1. What happened first in the story?

2. Think about the order in which things happened in the story. Use a chart to organize your ideas. Then retell the story.

Beginning	↓
Middle	↓
End	

3. Read the words wood, should, loved, and door. Use each one in a sentence.

4. Do you think it would be fun to work at an animal shelter? Why or why not?

Fly Away

by Ronda Greenberg

illustrated by Chad Thompson

PEARSON

Scott
Foresman

Editorial Offices: Glenview, Illinois • Parsippany, New Jersey • New York, New York
Sales Offices: Needham, Massachusetts • Duluth, Georgia • Glenview, Illinois
Coppell, Texas • Ontario, California • Mesa, Arizona

The boy and his dad went to meet the woman near a forest.

"Time to fly away," said the woman. The boy loved watching the owl fly high. They all waved. "Good-bye," they shouted.

8

ISBN: 0-328-13217-9

Copyright © Pearson Education, Inc.

All Rights Reserved. Printed in the United States of America. This publication is
protected by Copyright, and permission should be obtained from the publisher
prior to any prohibited reproduction, storage in a retrieval system, or transmission
in any form by any means, electronic, mechanical, photocopying, recording, or
likewise. For information regarding permission(s), write to: Permissions Department,
Scott Foresman, 1900 East Lake Avenue, Glenview, Illinois 60025.

2 3 4 5 6 7 8 9 10 V010 14 13 12 11 10 09 08 07 06 05

Many weeks passed. Finally the
owl could fly. His wing was better. He
should go back into the wild.
The woman called the boy who found
the owl. It was time to let the owl go.

7

The woman made sure the owl was resting and warm. She fixed its wing.

It was time to feed the owl. The woman gave the owl mice. Owls like mice.

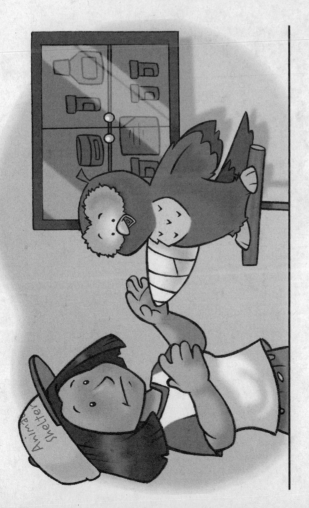

6

One day a boy was playing in his yard. He saw something near a pile of wood. It was an owl. The owl was hurt.

3

The boy yelled for his dad. His dad opened the door and came out.

His dad looked at the owl. Then he called an animal shelter. That's a place where you can take hurt animals.

4

A woman from the shelter came and looked at the owl. Its wing was broken.

The woman knew what to do. She put the owl in a cage and took it back to the shelter.

5

What Does a Detective Do?

by Juan Lester

illustrated by Donna Catanese

Suggested levels for Guided Reading, DRA,™
Lexile,® and Reading Recovery™ are provided
in the Pearson Scott Foresman Leveling Guide.

Genre	Comprehension Skills and Strategy
Realistic Fiction	• Compare and Contrast • Cause and Effect • Monitor and Fix Up

Scott Foresman Reading Street 1.5.3

PEARSON

Scott
Foresman

scottforesman.com

Vocabulary

among

another

instead

Word count: 128

Think and Share

Read Together

1. How are the paw prints of a cat and a dog alike? How are they different?

2. What do you do if you don't understand what you're reading?

3. Think of words you know that have the same vowel sound as look. Write them on a word-family ladder like this.

Word-Family Ladder
look

4. If Grandma broke the cookie jar, what clues might you find?

What Does a Detective Do?

by Juan Lester
illustrated by Donna Catanese

PEARSON
Scott Foresman

Editorial Offices: Glenview, Illinois • Parsippany, New Jersey • New York, New York
Sales Offices: Needham, Massachusetts • Duluth, Georgia • Glenview, Illinois
Coppell, Texas • Ontario, California • Mesa, Arizona

Different Kinds of Detectives Read Together

There are different kinds of detectives. Some are police officers. They help solve crimes.

Another type of detective is a private detective. People pay private detectives to find lost people and things.

Would you like to be a detective?

8

ISBN: 0-328-13220-9

Copyright © Pearson Education, Inc.

All Rights Reserved. Printed in the United States of America. This publication is protected by Copyright, and permission should be obtained from the publisher prior to any prohibited reproduction, storage in a retrieval system, or transmission in any form by any means, electronic, mechanical, photocopying, recording, or likewise. For information regarding permission(s), write to: Permissions Department, Scott Foresman, 1900 East Lake Avenue, Glenview, Illinois 60025.

2 3 4 5 6 7 8 9 10 V010 14 13 12 11 10 09 08 07 06 05

Did you see a cat go by?

I saw a yellow cat go that way.

Sometimes, you can't find a clue by just looking. There may be none around. Instead, you can ask people questions. This might lead you to the right answer.

7

Look at the picture. What do you see? Who do you think broke the cookie jar?

The paw prints by the broken cookie jar were a clue. A clue helps you tell what happened. Detectives always look for clues.

Was it the dog? Was it the cat? Was it Grandma or Joe? Look at the paw prints among the pieces of the cookie jar? Are the paw prints big or litle?

4

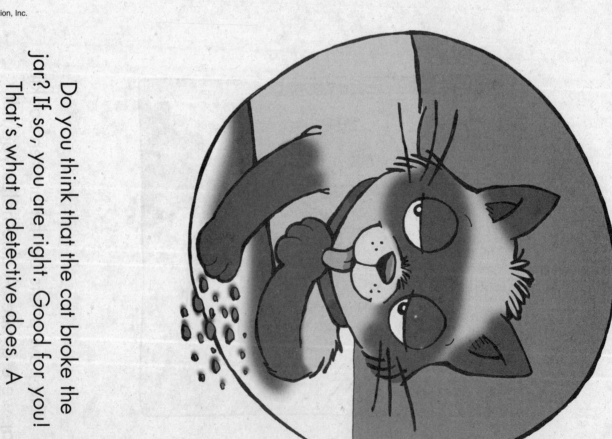

Do you think that the cat broke the jar? If so, you are right. Good for you! That's what a detective does. A detective works at figuring out what happened.

5

Physical Science

Science

Science

The Inclined Plane

by Mary Katherine Tate

Genre	Comprehension Skills and Strategy
Expository nonfiction	• Main Idea • Cause and Effect • Summarize

Scott Foresman Reading Street 1.5.4

PEARSON
Scott Foresman

scottforesman.com

ISBN 0-328-13223-3

9 780328 132232

90000

Vocabulary

against

goes

heavy

kinds

today

Word count: 237

Note: The total word count includes words in the running text and headings only. Numerals and words in chapter titles, captions, labels, diagrams, charts, graphs, sidebars, and extra features are not included.

Think and Share

1. What would be another good title for this book?

2. If someone who had not read this book asked you what it was about, what would you say?

3. Draw a picture of an inclined plane. Label your picture. Write a sentence to go with it. Use these words: *against, goes, heavy, kind.*

4. Think about inclined planes you have used. Describe some of them in a chart like this.

Inclined Plane	How I Used It
hill	pull up my sled

The Inclined Plane

by Mary Katherine Tate

PEARSON
Scott Foresman

Editorial Offices: Glenview, Illinois • Parsippany, New Jersey • New York, New York
Sales Offices: Needham, Massachusetts • Duluth, Georgia • Glenview, Illinois
Coppell, Texas • Ontario, California • Mesa, Arizona

People have been using inclined planes since long, long ago. Inclined planes are still helpful today.

12

Every effort has been made to secure permission and provide appropriate credit for photographic material. The publisher deeply regrets any omission and pledges to correct errors called to its attention in subsequent editions.

Unless otherwise acknowledged, all photographs are the property of Scott Foresman, a division of Pearson Education.

Photo locators denoted as follows: Top (T), Center (C), Bottom (B), Left (L), Right (R), Background (Bkgd)

1 ©Kelly-Mooney Photography/CORBIS; 7(B) ©Ann Giordano/CORBIS; 10 ©Kelly-Mooney Photography/CORBIS; 12 ©Dorling Kindersley Media Library

ISBN: 0-328-13223-3

© Pearson Education, Inc.

If you said walking up the ladder takes more energy, you are right. Inclined planes make it easier to move just about anything.

People often must move heavy things.
Movers move boxes. Builders move
lumber and tools. Drivers move things
with their trucks. All that moving is a lot
of work!

You can also use an inclined plane to
move yourself!
Which takes more energy—walking
up a slide ladder or going down the
slide?

4

There are many kinds of machines that help move things. Some are very simple. One simple machine is called an inclined plane.

You can use an inclined plane to move all kinds of things. The man in the picture below is pushing against the heavy crate to make it slide up the ramp.

9

An inclined plane has a flat surface.
It is higher on one end. An inclined plane
is used to move things up or down.

If you said push the box up the ramp,
you are right.
The ramp is an inclined plane, so it
helps you do the work.

Ramps are inclined planes. So is a road or a path that goes up a hill. Did you know that a slide is also an inclined plane?

6

Which is easier for the boy to do—lift up the box or push the box up the ramp?

7

Social Studies

The Telephone

by Marcus Jones

Genre	Comprehension Skills and Strategy	Text Features
Expository nonfiction	• Draw Conclusions • Author's Purpose • Monitor and Fix Up	• Captions

Scott Foresman Reading Street 1.5.5

ISBN 0-328-13226-8

90000

9 780328 132263

PEARSON
Scott Foresman

scottforesman.com

Vocabulary

built
early
learn
science
through

Word count: 167

Note: The total word count includes words in the running text and headings only. Numerals and words in chapter titles, captions, labels, diagrams, charts, graphs, sidebars, and extra features are not included.

Think and Share

Read Together

1. What can you say about Alexander Bell? Write a sentence about him.

2. Look back on page 7. Use a chart like the one below. List the steps you would follow to make a 9-1-1 call.

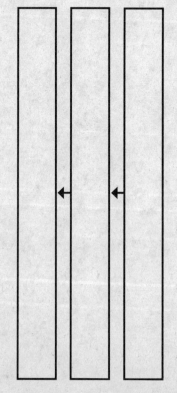

3. Find the word saw on page 6. Write three more words with the same vowel sound as saw spelled with aw.

4. Why is the telephone an important invention?

The Telephone

by Marcus Jones

PEARSON
Scott
Foresman

Editorial Offices: Glenview, Illinois • Parsippany, New Jersey • New York, New York
Sales Offices: Needham, Massachusetts • Duluth, Georgia • Glenview, Illinois
Coppell, Texas • Ontario, California • Mesa, Arizona

Are the roads open after a snowstorm?
Use the telephone to find out.

The telephone is also good for finding things out. For example, you can call your school and find out if it is open after a storm.

Telephones make our lives better.

Every effort has been made to secure permission and provide appropriate credit for photographic material. The publisher deeply regrets any omission and pledges to correct errors called to its attention in subsequent editions.

Unless otherwise acknowledged, all photographs are the property of Scott Foresman, a division of Pearson Education.

Photo locators denoted as follows: Top (T), Center (C), Bottom (B), Left (L), Right (R), Background (Bkgd)

Cover: ©Rob Lewine/Corbis; 3 ©Bettmann/Corbis; 4 ©Corbis; 5 ©Rob Lewine/Corbis; 6 ©Tom Stewart/Corbis; 8 ©Reuters/Corbis

ISBN: 0-328-13226-8

Dial 9-1-1 to get help.

The people who answer the phone at 9-1-1 will send help. Use your head. Tell them what the problem is. Do not hang up because they need to find out where you are.

7

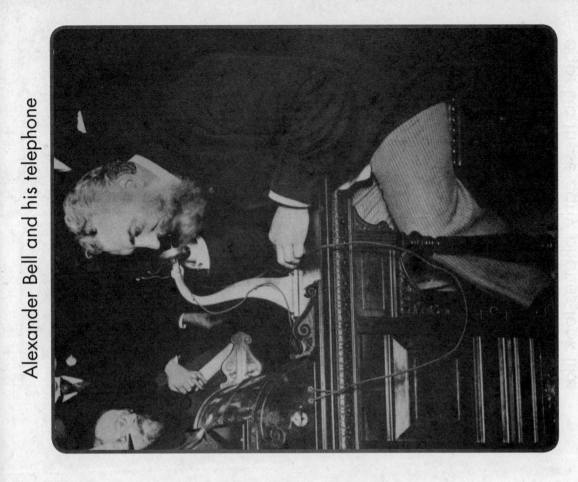

Alexander Bell and his telephone

Alexander Bell built a telephone in 1876. He had to learn a lot of science to do it.

The phone can be used to get help when someone is sick.

Using a phone is a big help if there is trouble or danger. For example, if you saw someone get hurt, you or a grown-up would dial 9-1-1.

Here are some telephones from long ago. Do these early phones look like your phone?

Phones use electricity to send calls. Some calls are sent through wires. Some calls are sent through the air.

Some phones can get calls that travel through air.

Using the phone is a great way to talk to friends and family. Who do you like to talk to on the phone?

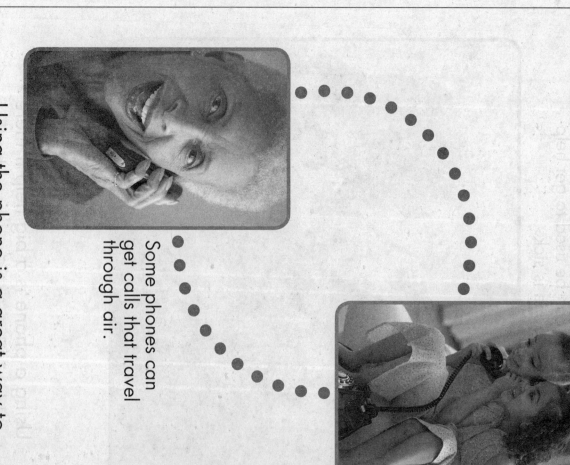

4

5

A Library
Comes to Town

by Juan Lester

illustrated by David Shelton

Suggested levels for Guided Reading, DRA,™ Lexile,® and Reading Recovery™ are provided in the Pearson Scott Foresman Leveling Guide.

Genre	Comprehension Skills and Strategy	
Historical fiction	• Theme • Sequence • Ask Questions	

Scott Foresman Reading Street 1.5.6

PEARSON

Scott Foresman

scottforesman.com

ISBN 0-328-13229-2

9 780328 132294

90000

Vocabulary

answered

brothers

carry

different

poor

Word count: 136

Think and Share (Read Together)

1. What is the big idea of this story?

2. What questions would you ask Ben Franklin about his idea for a library?

3. On a separate sheet of paper, write the words from the story that begin with un-. Use the words in a sentence.

4. Benjamin Franklin started the first library in the United States. How do people use libraries today? Fill in a web like this one.

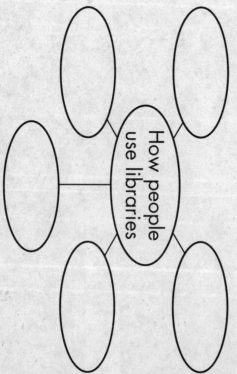

How people use libraries

A **Library** Comes to Town

by Juan Lester

illustrated by David Shelton

PEARSON
Scott
Foresman

Editorial Offices: Glenview, Illinois • Parsippany, New Jersey • New York, New York
Sales Offices: Needham, Massachusetts • Duluth, Georgia • Glenview, Illinois
Coppell, Texas • Ontario, California • Mesa, Arizona

Ben Franklin

Ben Franklin opened up the first public library in the United States. This was more than 200 years ago. He wanted to make sure that everyone could have books to read. He also came up with other "firsts."

Ben Franklin invented swimming fins, a stove, and a special kind of reading glasses. All these are things that people still use today.

Every effort has been made to secure permission and provide appropriate credit for photographic material. The publisher deeply regrets any omission and pledges to correct errors called to its attention in subsequent editions.

Unless otherwise acknowledged, all photographs are the property of Scott Foresman, a division of Pearson Education.

8 ©Bettmann/CORBIS

ISBN: 0-328-13229-2

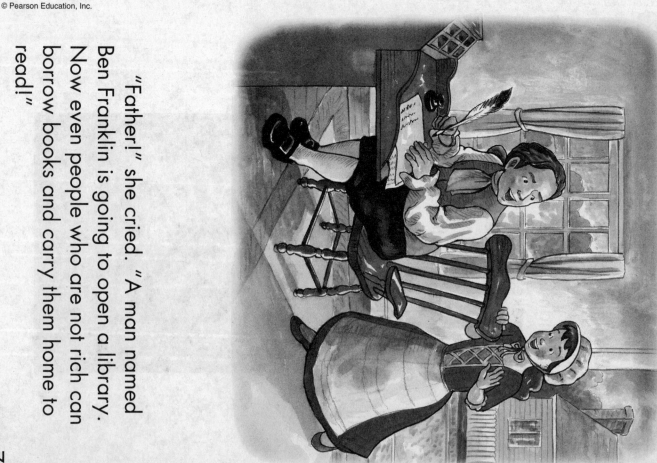

"Father!" she cried. "A man named Ben Franklin is going to open a library. Now even people who are not rich can borrow books and carry them home to read!"

Jane and her father looked in a bookstore window. Father sighed.

"Why are you unhappy?" asked Jane.

A week later, Jane was helping her brothers repaint some old chairs. She could hear some neighbors talking.

What she heard made her happy. She went running to tell her father.

4

"Oh, child, I love to read all different kinds of books," answered Father. "But books cost a lot of money."

"Are we too poor to buy books?" asked Jane.

"No, but we are not rich enough to buy most books," said Father. "I wish there were a way that everyone could have books to read," said Jane.

5